A first guide to

◆

China

By Kath Davies

A ZOË BOOK

A ZOË BOOK

© 1995 Zoë Books Limited

Devised and produced by
Zoë Books Limited
15 Worthy Lane
Winchester
Hampshire SO23 7AB
England

Illustrative material used in this book first appeared in *Discovering China*, published by Zoë Books Limited.

First published in Great Britain in 1995 by
Zoë Books Limited
15 Worthy Lane
Winchester
Hampshire SO23 7AB

A record of the CIP data is available from the British Library.

ISBN 1 874488 36 3

Printed in Italy by Grafedit SpA
Design: Jan Sterling, Sterling Associates
Editor: Denise Allard
Picture research: Victoria Sturgess
Map: Gecko Limited
Production: Grahame Griffiths

Photographic acknowledgments
The publishers wish to acknowledge, with thanks, the following photographic sources:

Cover: The Hutchison Library/Christine Pemberton; Title page: Zefa; 5 Robert Harding Picture Library; 6 The Hutchison Library/John Egan; 7l The Hutchison Library/Christina Dodwell; 7r, 8 Robert Harding Picture Library; 9l The Hutchison Library/Dave Brinicombe; 9r The Hutchison Library; 10 Bruce Coleman Ltd/WWF/Kojo Tanaka; 11l The Hutchison Library/Jeremy Horner; 11r, 12 Robert Harding Picture Library; 13l & r The Hutchison Library; 14 Robert Harding Picture Library; 15l The Hutchison Library/Trevor Page; 15r Bruce Coleman Ltd/Orion Service and Trading Co. Inc; 16 Ancient Art and Architecture Collection; 17l The Hutchison Library/ Melanie Friend; 17r, 18, 19l & r Robert Harding Picture Library; 20 The Hutchison Library/ Christine Pemberton; 21l The Hutchison Library/Felix Greene; 21r, 22, 23l & r Robert Harding Picture Library; 24 Michael Holford; 25l Ancient Art and Architecture Collection; 25r Robert Harding Picture Library; 26, 27l Peter Newark's Historical Pictures; 27r The Mansell Collection; 28 Peter Newark's Historical Pictures; 29l & r Robert Harding Picture Library.

Cover: *The Temple of Heaven, in the Forbidden City, Beijing*

Title Page: *The Great Wall of China*

Contents

Chinese words are shown in *italics* and are explained in the text.

4

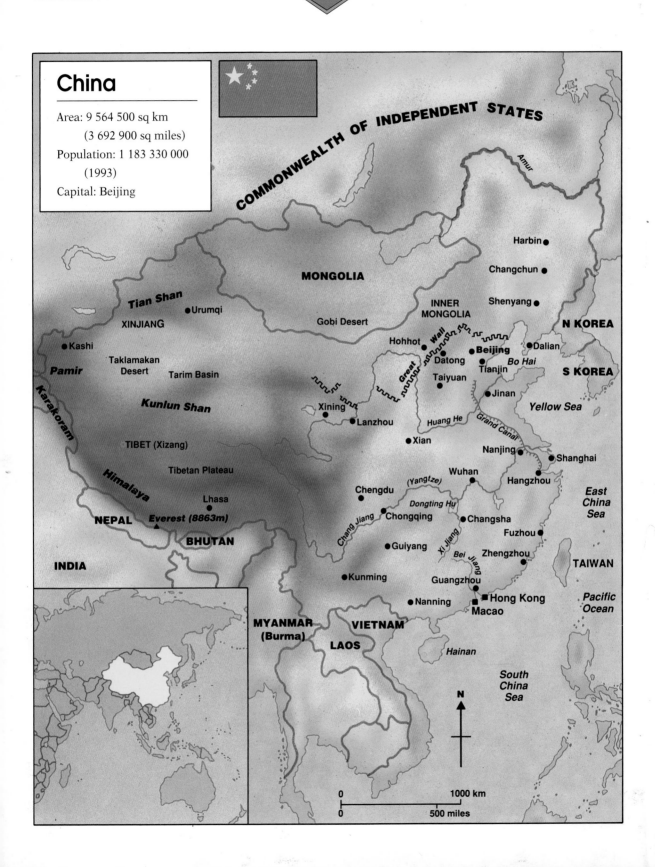

China

Area: 9 564 500 sq km
(3 692 900 sq miles)
Population: 1 183 330 000
(1993)
Capital: Beijing

COMMONWEALTH OF INDEPENDENT STATES

Amur

MONGOLIA

Tian Shan

Urumqi

XINJIANG

Gobi Desert

Harbin

Changchun

Shenyang

INNER MONGOLIA

N KOREA

Kashi

Hohhot

Great Wall

Beijing

Dalian

Taklamakan Desert

Tarim Basin

Datong

Tianjin

Bo Hai

S KOREA

Pamir

Kunlun Shan

Xining

Taiyuan

Jinan

Yellow Sea

Karakoram

Lanzhou

Huang He

Grand Canal

TIBET (Xizang)

Xian

Nanjing

Shanghai

Tibetan Plateau

Wuhan

Hangzhou

East China Sea

Himalaya

Lhasa

Chengdu

(Yangtze)

Everest (8863m)

Chang Jiang

Dongting Hu

Chongqing

Changsha

Fuzhou

NEPAL

BHUTAN

Guiyang

Xi Jiang

Zhengzhou

TAIWAN

INDIA

Kunming

Bei Jiang

Guangzhou

Nanning

Hong Kong

Macao

Pacific Ocean

MYANMAR (Burma)

VIETNAM

LAOS

Hainan

South China Sea

N

0   1000 km
0   500 miles

Welcome to China!

More than one thousand million people live in China. That is more than in any other country on Earth. There are the Han Chinese people, the Hui and the Miao, as well as many other groups.

Most children learn the Chinese language called Mandarin at school. 'Hello!' in Mandarin is '*Ni hao*!'

A huge land

China is a huge land. It is almost as large as Europe. The east and the south of China are very crowded. In the west and the north there are deserts and high mountains. Not many people can live here.

To the north of China lie the snowy forests of Siberia, in Russia. To the south are the hot tropical lands of India and Southeast Asia. The seas around China are part of the Pacific Ocean.

▲ A Miao girl

The winds from the Pacific Ocean bring violent storms called typhoons.

Lands of the south

The southeast of China is very beautiful. There are mountains, hills and plains. The climate is warm and wet. People grow fruit such as pineapples and lychees. They also grow rice and tea, and they fish along the coasts. Visitors come to the tropical beaches of Hainan island.

There are old and new industries in this area. People make silk, and wooden furniture called lacquer, which is coloured and varnished. There are electronics and chemical industries in the cities.

The biggest southern city is called Guangzhou, or Canton. Its skyscrapers rise above streets full of people, buses and bicycles.

▼ A peaceful scene in southern China

▲ The limestone pillars of Shilin

The land of spring

The province of Yunnan is in southwest China. The climate there is warm, like spring. The city of Kunming has a lake, and green parks with flowers and goldfish ponds.

People travel by bus to see the strange rocks at Shilin. The rocks are called the Stone Forest.

In the real forest, further south, there are tigers and peacocks.

China's government

China is divided into five large areas, or regions. There are 21 smaller areas, called provinces, and three city areas, or municipalities. The Chinese island of Taiwan has its own government.

Parts of China have been ruled by other countries for many years. Macao is on the southeast coast. It is ruled by Portugal, but in 1999 it will be returned to China. Hong Kong is ruled by Britain. It will be returned to China in 1997.

▼ Hong Kong's harbour

On top of the world

The highest mountains in the world are the Himalayas. They lie on the southwestern border of China. The land of Tibet is called the 'roof of the world'. China rules Tibet. The Chinese name for Tibet is Xizang. Tibet has its own language, history and customs. It was once an independent country.

▼ The palace of Potala, in Lhasa

▲ On the old 'Silk Road'

The religion of many Tibetan people is Buddhism. Their leader, the Dalai Lama, used to live in the Potala palace, in Lhasa. Now he lives abroad.

The Silk Road

For thousands of years, people carried goods on camels and mules across the mountains of northwest China. They were taking silk and tea to sell in Arabia and in Europe. These traders were often attacked by bandits. Today, buses and trucks drive along the old Silk Road.

The northwest

In the region of Xinjiang, there are deserts and mountains. The summers are very hot and dry. Water is brought from the mountains, so that crops such as fruit and corn can grow.

The people who live in the northwest of China are called the Tajiks and the Uzbeks. They follow the faith of Islam.

▼ Calling the Muslims to prayer

Sichuan to Shanghai

The bamboo plant grows on the mountains of Sichuan province. It is food for the giant panda. The pandas are now protected, because they were in danger of dying out.

The rivers of Sichuan join the river Chang Jiang. It is the third longest river in the world, at 6300 kilometres (3937 miles). Part of the river is called the Yangtze.

▼ Giant pandas live in southwest China

▲ River boats at the Gezhouba lock

The biggest city in Sichuan is Chongqing. It has many factories. From Chongqing, boats of all sizes carry people or goods such as coal along the Chang Jiang river.

The river flows through rocky gorges. The water turns huge engines in the Gezhouba Dam. These engines are used to make electricity. The boats pass through a deep lock to reach the lower part of the river. Here the Chang Jiang river flows through the rich farmland of Hunan and Hubei.

The Grand Canal

The Grand Canal took almost 2000 years to build, and was finished in AD1327. Boats carried rice along the canal, from the south to the north of China. The southern part of the canal is still busy today.

Shanghai

The great sea port of Shanghai lies on the southeast coast. Today, Shanghai is the largest city in China. About 13 million people live there. It has shipyards and steelworks, and factories which make television sets and household goods.

▼ The bright lights of Shanghai

Yellow earth

In the high, flat, central and northern areas of China, the soil is a yellow-brown colour. It is called 'loess'. The wind blew this soil from the deserts in the north.

▲ The muddy waters of the Huang He River

The long river which winds through this part of China is called the Huang He, or the Yellow River. The river used to flood in the rainy seasons. It washed yellow mud on to the land. Now dams and banks of earth stop the river from flooding. People grow crops such as vegetables, wheat and maize in the rich, muddy soil.

Northern cities

The city of Xi'an, in Shaanxi province, was once the capital of China. It has old city walls, tall towers, and pagodas.

There are also modern mills and factories in Xi'an. Coal, iron and steel come from this part of China. People make trucks, carpets, household goods and machinery.

Tianjin is a busy seaport, where eight million people live.

▼ Steel is made in a blast furnace

▲ A steam train in China

Travel by rail

Most trains in China are pulled by diesel engines, but there are still some steam engines. These are made in the town of Datong, in Shanxi province.

Not many people in China own cars, so rail travel is very important. Some trains are very crowded. On long journeys, people can buy food and tea. They can also sleep on the trains, in bunks.

The journey from China to Moscow, in Russia, usually takes six days!

The far north

The Mongol people live in the Chinese region called Inner Mongolia. The Mongol people have their own languages and customs. Many of them follow the Buddhist faith.

Inner Mongolia is a wide, grassy land. It is very hot in summer, and freezing cold in winter. The people raise camels, sheep, goats and cattle. They are very good horse riders. Many people now live in villages and towns. There are factories and steelworks in cities such as Hohhot and Baotou.

▼ On the grasslands in Mongolia

The northeast

The old name for the northeast was Manchuria. The winters here are icy, but in summer crops grow, such as sugar beet, maize and soya beans. Forests provide timber for building.

Coal, iron and copper are mined here, and there is oil at Daqing. The northeast is now one of China's most important industrial centres. The people make cars, trucks, paper and chemicals.

▼ Building a wooden house

▲ Japanese cranes

In the wilds

The rare Manchurian tiger lives in the northeast. Other animals such as the red deer, the brown bear and the lynx also live here. The long-legged bird called the crane makes its home here too.

Many rare animals are now threatened, because the forests are being cut down, and new villages are being built. There are now more than three hundred nature reserves in China. Wildlife is protected in these nature reserves.

Beijing

The capital city of China is called Beijing. It is in the north of the country. About 11 million people live in Beijing. The streets are crowded with bicycles, buses, horses and carts. There are many new hotels and high-rise flats in the city.

▲ The Palace of Heavenly Purity in the Forbidden City

▲ The modern city of Beijing

The old city

The Imperial Palace is at the centre of the old city. The Chinese royal family lived here, behind high red walls. Ordinary people were not allowed to enter the palace area. It was called the Forbidden City.

The government

The Communist Party of China rules the country. Laws are made by the National People's Congress, in Beijing. Some members of the Congress come from the Chinese provinces.

What to see

The fine Summer Palace stands amongst lakes and hills. In Beihai Park, people go boating and skating on the lakes.

Many people visit the tomb of the Chinese leader, Mao Zedong. It is near Tiananmen Square.

One of the finest buildings in China is the Temple of Heaven, *Tiantan*. The rulers prayed here for good crops. The temple was built more than 500 years ago.

▼ The roof of the Temple of Heaven

All in a day's work

It is hard work to feed all the people who live in China. Chinese farmers must grow food even where the soil is not good, or the climate is harsh. The farmers work in flooded rice fields, in hot sun and in the cold winters.

▲ Women work in the rice fields

All the workers in a village, or commune, used to work together. The government told people how to grow and sell the crops. Today there are some independent farmers. They can sell some of their crops at the local village markets, as well as in the bigger cities.

▲ Lessons in a village school

Working families

In most families, women and men go out to work. Women as well as men work on farms, in shops, schools, factories, hotels, hospitals, and in the army.

Keeping in touch

Many people now come to visit China. Some visitors sail to China from Hong Kong. Other people fly into Beijing.

The large cities in China have airports. There are many roads, but some of the country highways are bumpy!

Working for health

There are modern hospitals in China's towns and cities. In the country, there are small clinics. Many Chinese medicines are made from plants, or herbs.

A cure called acupuncture is very popular. Needles are put into special places in a person's body. They help people to feel better.

▼ Acupuncture keeps people healthy

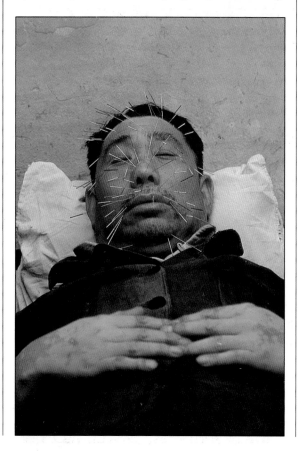

At home

Houses and flats in Chinese towns are often very crowded. Families sometimes share kitchens or courtyards. Children, parents and grandparents may live together. Grandparents often look after children while parents work.

The number of people in China is growing fast. Every day 44 000 babies are born. The Chinese government would like families not to have more than one or two children.

▼ Flats in the large town of Datong

▲ A Chinese family eating dinner

Mealtime in China

People in China eat rice or noodles at most meals.

At midday or in the evening, there may be fish or meat. Fresh vegetables such as onions, peppers and mushrooms are very popular. Soup is served at the end of a meal. People use chopsticks instead of knives and forks.

People mostly eat at home. However, popular snacks such as pancakes, dumplings, sweets and ice cream are often bought from street stalls. People drink tea with all meals, and they also enjoy beer.

Food around China

Each region of China has its own special dishes.

Beijing is famous for its crispy duck. Dishes from the north use bean sauce, oil and garlic.

Light sauces, fresh fish, ham and vegetables are popular in eastern China. In Sichuan, food is hot and spicy. People cook with ginger, garlic and chili.

Cantonese cooking includes sweet-and-sour pork and dumplings called *dim sum*. A dish of lamb dipped in sauces comes from Inner Mongolia.

▼ A street stall in Chongqing

Sports and the arts

People enjoy swimming, athletics, football, table tennis, basketball, gymnastics and volley-ball. Some older sports, such as wrestling, archery and horse-riding, are also popular. In 1990, the Asian Games were held in Beijing.

Everyone likes to keep fit! People practise movements called *taijiquan*, or 'tai chi', and run in the parks. Others learn the way of fighting called *gongu*, or 'kung fu'.

Kite-flying is popular, and so are games of chess and cards. People also enjoy dancing.

▼ 'Tai chi' exercises in Shanghai

▲ Dragon dancers at a festival

Holidays and festivals

The Spring Festival is the most important holiday in the year. It is held in January, on the day of a New Moon. There is dancing in the streets, and families visit each other. Weddings are often held at the Spring Festival.

Another spring holiday is the Lantern Festival, and in summer there is the Dragon Boat Festival.

Children's Day is 1 June, and Women's Day is 8 March. China's National Day is held on 1 October.

Arts, crafts and music

Chinese poetry is written with a brush and ink. This art is called calligraphy.

The Chinese were the first people to make silk, and fine dishes (called 'china', or porcelain). They carve a green stone called jade into jewellery and figures.

The actors and singers in Chinese opera wear bright costumes. At the theatre, there are conjuring shows and acrobats.

▼ An actress in a Chinese opera

China long ago

People have lived in China for about 600 000 years. The remains of these prehistoric people have been found near Beijing.

About 7000 years ago, people came to live near the Yellow River. They fished and hunted and learned how to farm. There is a village near Xi'an, at Banpo, which was built about 5000 years ago. The people grew crops, kept animals and made pottery.

▼ A carving of a man and a tiger

The Shang royal family ruled 3000 years ago. The people of that time knew how to write and how to make silk. They also made tools from a metal called bronze.

The Zhou family overthrew the Shang rulers, and called themselves the 'Sons of Heaven'. Two great teachers lived at this time. They were Lao Zi (Lao Tse) and Kong Fuzi (Confucius). Their ideas became the religions called Taoism and Confucianism.

▲ The emperor's underground army

A buried army

About 2500 years ago, many small states in China fought each other. Then the country united under the emperor Qin Shi Huangdi. When he died, thousands of clay or bronze soldiers were buried with him. They were found in 1974.

The Han family ruled the united empire for about 400 years. China traded with other countries, and it was a time of new ideas and inventions. The religion of Buddhism came to China from India.

The Great Wall

For more than a thousand years, slaves and soldiers worked to build this wall. They began about 2300 years ago. The wall kept China's enemies out, and it was also a road across the country. The wall now stretches for about 3460 km (2162 miles). Once it may have been 10 000 km (6250 miles) long.

▼ The Great Wall of China

The Middle Kingdom

Chinese people once believed that China was the middle of the world. They thought that their way of life was more advanced than life in the countries around them.

During the time of the Tang and the Song dynasties, 1300 to 700 years ago, the Chinese people were right. When the Mongols invaded China, they lived in the Chinese way. The Mongol emperor of China at that time was Kublai Khan.

▼ Marco Polo at the court of Kublai Khan

▲ The British attack in 1841

The explorer Marco Polo visited Kublai Khan. He returned to Europe to tell people about the wonders which he had seen in China.

From 1368 until 1644 the Ming family ruled. Chinese ships carried silk, tea and other goods to Asia and Africa.

Foreigners and rebels

The Qing family were the last royal rulers of China. The world was changing. Britain and Portugal now used China's trade routes, and Britain sold the drug opium to China. In 1839, after the 'opium war', the Chinese gave up Hong Kong to Britain.

China was no longer a great power. In 1853 and in 1900 there were rebellions against the rulers.

The great empress

Sometimes the person who came to the throne was a child. An adult, called a regent, had to rule until the child grew up. The empress Cixi was a regent. She was very powerful.

The last Chinese emperor, Puyi, was a small boy. He ruled until 1911.

▼ Empress Cixi in 1903

New worlds

In 1911 there was another rebellion in China. It ended the rule of the emperors. Since that time, China has been ruled by the people. It is now a republic.

In the last 80 years, many people have had different ideas about how to govern China. The Nationalist Party, the *Guomindang*, was led by Chiang Kai Shek (Jiang Jieshi). The Nationalists sometimes worked with the Communist Party, but they also fought each other.

During the Second World War, the Communists fought the Japanese and the Nationalists. In 1949, they defeated the Nationalist Party.

▲ The Chinese leader, Mao Zedong, with his soldiers in 1947

▲ Red Guards in Tiananmen Square, Beijing

Communism in China

In October 1949, the new People's Republic of China was formed. Its leader was Mao Zedong. Life in China changed. New industries were set up and people worked together on large farms.

In 1966, Mao's ideas were called the 'Cultural Revolution'. Young people joined a group called the Red Guards. They wanted to support the new ideas. People who disagreed with the changes were often attacked or put in prison.

Today and tomorrow

The leader, Deng Xiaoping, made many changes to life in China. Today it is easier to visit China, and for Chinese people to travel to other countries.

Some people have protested because they want more say in their government. In 1989 many students were killed in Tiananmen Square.

Young people in China are now looking forward to the twenty-first century.

▼ Beijing today

Fact file

Flag and anthem

The Chinese flag is red, for revolution. It shows the star of communism.

China's national song, or anthem, is *The March of the Volunteers*. It was written by Nie Er in 1935.

Money

In China, money is called 'the people's money'. One *yuan* is made up of 10 *jiaou* or 100 *fen*.

Religion

Some people's religion is based on Taoism or Confucianism. Other people are Christians, Muslims or Buddhists.

Education

There are two terms in the Chinese school year. Children go to infant school and primary school. At 13, they start junior middle school, then at 16 there is senior middle school. Students then go on to college or start work.

Chinese writing

The Chinese language has about 50 000 characters! When Chinese is written using letters, it is called *Pinyin*.

The media

The People's Daily is the main Chinese newspaper. The *China Daily* is printed in English. There is one national TV channel for all China and there are many local channels. Cinemas are very popular in China.

Naming the years

Each Chinese new year has a different name. 1995 is the year of the Pig, 1996 is the Rat and 1997 the Ox. The year 2000 will be the year of the Dragon.

Some famous people

Lao Tse (born c.604BC) was a thinker, or philosopher.

Confucius (551-479BC) was a philosopher at court.

Qin Shi Huangdi (died 210BC), the first emperor of all China.

Pan Chao (c.AD45-115), the most famous Chinese female scholar.

Wu (died AD705) was an empress who supported Buddhism.

Wang Wei (699-759) was a painter.

Kublai Khan (1215-94) was a Mongol emperor of China.

Zheng He (lived in the 1400s) was an admiral and a navigator.

Cixi (1835-1908) was an empress and regent.

Sun Yatsen (1866-1925) formed the Chinese Republic.

Chiang Kai-Shek (1887-1975) was president of China.

Mao Zedong (1893-1976) was Chairman of the Chinese Communist Party.

Some key events in history

7000BC: farming started in northern China.

1122BC: the Shang dynasty was overthrown.

300BC: work began on the Great Wall of China.

221BC: Qin Shi Huangdi ruled over all China.

AD65: Buddhism came to China.

960: the Song dynasty ruled.

1260: Kublai Khan became emperor of China.

1368: the Ming dynasty ruled.

1421: Beijing became the capital of China.

1644: the Manchu invaded.

1839: the first Opium War.

1911: the founding of the Chinese republic.

1937-45: war with Japan.

1946-49: civil war.

1966-69: the Cultural Revolution.

1971: China joined the United Nations.

Index